The Man Who Rode the Tiger

Retold by Beverley Randell

Illustrated by Pat Reynolds

Chapter One

The Endless Dripping

Once upon a time, far away in India, a storm went on for days. The wind blew, the lightning flashed, and the rain came pouring down.

Water dripped through the roof of an old house. The poor woman who lived there ran back and forth as she tried to catch the drips in her cooking bowls.

"Will these drips never stop?" she cried. "How I hate them! I'm not frightened of thunder and lightning, but this endless dripping is driving me mad!"

She wept and wailed as she pushed her bed away from the drips. "I'm not frightened of fierce tigers, or crawling snakes, or wild elephants," she shouted. "But this endless dripping is horrible. How I wish it would go away!"

The poor woman didn't know that a tiger was sheltering beside her house, listening to everything she said.

The tiger thought that the "endless dripping" was a wild animal! He shivered with fright. "What does the **Endless Dripping** look like?" he wondered. "It must be more terrifying than elephants, or snakes—or even tigers!"

Just at that moment, a potter came walking along. He was wet to the skin, and very angry because his donkey had run away. When the potter saw the dark shape of the tiger sheltering from the rain, he thought that he had found his donkey. He crept up behind the tiger and grabbed him by the ears.

"I'm caught," thought the tiger. "The horrible **Endless Dripping** has caught me!"

The tiger was terrified. He was even more terrified when the potter climbed on his back and rode him down the village street!

The night was so dark and the rain was so heavy that the potter didn't notice that he was riding a tiger! He tied the beast to a post outside his house and went to bed.

Chapter Two

Everyone Is Astonished

The next morning, the potter's wife saw the tiger. "Do you know what beast you brought home in the storm last night?" she shrieked to her husband.

When the potter saw the tiger, he gasped. He could not believe what he had done!

The potter's wife told everyone in the village that her brave husband had ridden home on a tiger. "Look," she cried, "he even tied the tiger up!"

That very day, the rajah who ruled the kingdom came to see the astonishing sight. The rajah gave the potter a bag of gold as a reward, and his men carried the tiger away to the palace in a cage.

Chapter Three

The Potter Rides a Warhorse

Soon after that, the rajah's enemies decided to attack his kingdom. They had a large army of soldiers and horses, and they set up a camp near the border of the kingdom.

The rajah sent for his captains, who were trembling with fear. "What can we do?" asked the rajah.

"The man who rode the tiger is brave enough to save us all," said the captains.

So the rajah sent for the potter. "You are afraid of nothing!" said the rajah. "You can drive our enemies away. I will give you a warhorse, and put you in charge of my army."

The potter's knees shook when he saw the huge warhorse. He did not dare tell the rajah that he had never ridden a horse in his life!

The potter had to think of an excuse. "First let me say good-bye to my wife," he said. "Then tonight, when it is dark, I will spy on the enemy for you."

But that evening, before the potter could leave, on foot, to spy on the camp, the rajah sent his servants to the potter's house, with the enormous warhorse.

"You will just have to learn to ride it," said the potter's wife. "We can't send it back to the rajah. Pretend that it is a donkey."

"But it's impossible!" said the potter. "I can't even climb up on its back. It's much too high. Just look at it!"

"You will have to leap up," said his wife. "Go on, jump! No one will see you in the dark."

But when the potter jumped, he landed on the horse the wrong way around, facing its tail! The horse reared up, and the potter fell off, head first.

The potter tried again and again until, at last, he managed to sit on the saddle, facing the horse's head.

"I'll fall off again," cried the terrified potter. "I know I will."

"I'll tie you on firmly," said the potter's wife. She tied her husband's legs to the stirrups, and wound the rope around the horse's body. She used a second rope to tie his waist to the horse's neck.

Then the horse bolted away, with the potter clinging tightly to its mane. All night long, the horse galloped through fields, past villages, and over streams.

The potter had no idea where he was going. When the sun rose, he grabbed at a small tree as they dashed along, hoping to stop the horse and end the frantic ride. But the ground was soft, and the tree came out by the roots. The potter yelled with despair.

Just at that moment, the rajah's enemies came in sight. Hundreds of men on horseback were trotting forward.

Chapter Four

The Potter Is a Hero

When the soldiers saw the potter charging toward them on a mighty warhorse, yelling and waving a tree, they were terrified.

"A giant is coming!" they shrieked. "A whole army might be following him! We cannot fight an army of giants!" So every man turned his horse around and galloped for home.

The rajah's warhorse was frightened by all the noise, and it reared up. The ropes gave way, and the potter tumbled down beside the empty tents.

"They've all gone!" the potter exclaimed, as he looked around. "What a bit of luck!"

He knew that it was no use trying to ride the horse again. He caught it by the reins, and started to walk back to tell the rajah that his enemies had fled.

News of the great victory reached the rajah long before the potter arrived at the palace.

A crowd of people gathered to cheer him. "What a wonderful person he is," they said. "You would think that such a hero would ride home proudly on his horse. But look—here he comes, on foot, just like an ordinary man."

The grateful rajah gave the potter gold, and houses, and land.

And so the man who rode the tiger lived happily ever after.